MARCUS L. BOSTON

THE JOY
of the
LORD

- DAILY DEVOTIONAL -

UNFAZED PUBLISHING
YOUR MIND IS OUR BUSINESS

TAMPA FLORIDA

Marcus L. Boston

ISBN: 978-1-959275-25-1

Unless otherwise noted, all scripture is from the King James Version of the Bible.

Library of Congress Number 2023930266

Marcus L. Boston

Making The Church

A Better Place

Marcus L. Boston

UNFAZED PUBLISHING
YOUR MIND IS OUR BUSINESS

THE JOY OF THE LORD!

THE JOY OF THE LORD!

Joy: to fill with ecstatic happiness, pleasure, or satisfaction. To enjoy.

The Free Dictionary by Farlex

Introduction

Now that this book is completely, I had to come back to this section to add this. I had no clue this book would go in this direction. When God placed this book in my heart, I saw it one way, but God caused this book to go exactly how He desired. I understand my joy better now. It makes perfect sense to me now.

I write this book with an understanding of what it is to be alive and desire to be dead. I know how it feels to be surrounded by lots of people, and feel as if I am completely alone. I know what it's like to see life through sadness while being in the church. I've been isolated and suicidal. I had no desire to do anything I know I loved doing. I understand a life filled with disappointments with the Lord.

Here's what I've experienced as a Christian: depression, rejection, being lied on by Christians, abused over the pulpit, controlled by prophecy, slandered, lied on publicly on social media, wrongfully rebuked based on false information, and many other things. The Lord has helped me overcome these situations and circumstances. Moreover, the Lord taught me His joy through it all. I write this book with an understanding of how life really is in the Christian Church, and how Christians can be some of the nastiest, dirtiest, and most scandalous people on earth. Evil hearts exist in our churches although they shouldn't. Jesus said let the wheat and tare grow together, and He will do the separating. I know I don't want to be a tare. Jesus said He will also separate the goats and the sheep. I desire my name to be in the Lambs book of life. I desire an eternity with Jesus. I have forgiven many evils purposely executed against my life. I didn't receive an apology for most of them. No closure. Yes, I wanted revenge, but thank God I was seeking His face. God has taught me so much and I had to let those evil things done against me go.

Jesus experienced many things He didn't deserve. The Lord helped me forgive. I prayed and asked Him to help me forgive my enemies. It was very hard, but God helped me. I pray this book deals with your heart and brings you to a higher place in the Lord where His joy lives in you no matter what happens.

By the way, each day starts with you. For example, if you need a few days before you move on to the next day, please take your time. If you need to meditate and focus on a certain day in this book, please do so. Your heart may need to be before the Lord several days before you move on to the next day. God bless you.

-Day 1-

Joy In Forgiveness

Most of us, when we first received Jesus as our savior, were given these verses in Romans chapter 10 verses 9 and 10. KJV

"That if thou shalt confess with thy mouth the Lord Jesus, and shalt believe in thine heart that God hath raised him from the dead, thou shalt be saved. For with the heart, man believeth unto righteousness; and with the mouth confession is made unto salvation."

When we received Jesus as our savior, a change in our heart was established. This is greatest immediate change that takes place in our lives as we go from darkness into His marvelous light. We are now in the body of Christ and within the Kingdom of God. We will now spend eternity with Jesus, and this is something we should always celebrate. On day one, remember the day of your salvation. Remember the day you gave your life to Christ. "For by grace are ye saved through faith; and that not of yourselves: it is the gift of God: Not of works, lest any man should boast." Ephesians 2 v. 8 and 9

We should have joy because we are forgiven of our sins and forgiven of all our evil doings. We are loved by the creator of all things, and we should always be mindful of the price the Lord paid for us on the cross. We are forgiven of our sins and let me shed some light on something. When Jesus died for our sins and rose with all power in His Hands, His gift of grace that we have received covers our entire life. What does this mean? Jesus being all knowing died for every sin He knew we were going to commit throughout our entire lifetime. There is no new sin to Jesus. He died for it all! When I was first saved, I wasn't taught about God's grace. I was taught about works. I lived in guilt and condemnation because of the sins I was committing. I felt as if Jesus was angry with me and wasn't pleased. Please read my book, "A Pastor's Mistake. A Transparent Novel Testimony." I share my testimony in complete transparency. We are not to sin purposely, but the grace of God is for all of our sins and wrong doings. Never think the Lord is angry with you. If you're a new Christian, pray at home, read your bible, and learn to give God praise and worship daily. You will grow in grace. Keep asking God to help you do better. For you seasoned vets in the Lord, be at peace as well. Many of you wasn't taught the grace of God. For some of you, it's even hard reading this now. God has no respect of persons. Whether you're completely whole in the Lord and delivered, or whether you're a new Christian with tons of issues you're dealing with, God doesn't love you any less than He loves the strong Christians who have lived this life for many years. Apostle Paul, in my opinion, is the greatest Apostle ever. We are the fruit of his ministry. We are Christians today because of his assignments from the Lord. The Lord allowed Paul to be given a fault by the messenger of satan in 2nd Corinthians chapter 12 verse 7 – 10. Paul wanted it removed, but Jesus said unto him, "My grace is sufficient for thee: for my strength is made perfect in weakness." There will always be something in your life that you will need the grace of God for. This goes for the strongest looking ministers of the gospel. I don't need discernment to know there's something in your life that you need grace for. Apostle Paul is the only example I need. Because we all need the grace of God, we should walk in love towards each other no matter what any of us are dealing with or guilty of, "considering ourselves" as Galatian chapter 6 verse 1 explains. It might just be us that mess up big time needing some grace, love, and restoration in the Lord. Always put yourself in their shoes, (considering yourself) knowing that if you're very critical and judge them, you'll reap it if it's you one day. Love is the answer.

One thing is certain: you will need the grace of God for your entire life. As you grow in the Lord, you will need His grace to stand and endure many things as you seek to complete the assignments He has for you. Grace isn't just for salvation, it's for everything we do in the Lord. Nonetheless, no matter what happens in your Christian walk, just know you can always do what Hebrews chapter 4 verse 16 declares, "Let us therefore come boldly unto the throne of grace that we may obtain mercy, and find grace to help in the time of need." You can freely go before God in repentance as often as you need no matter what it's concerning. 1st John chapter 1 verse 9 says, "If we confess our sins, he is faithful and just to forgive us our sins, and to cleanse us from all unrighteousness." Why is Jesus so faithful to forgive us? Because He died for all our sins. I said it before, and I will repeat it just for you. When Jesus died for all our sins, He died for every sin we will ever commit throughout our entire life. Our job is to confess it, repent, and ask for forgiveness.

The forgiveness of our sins is priceless. Knowing Jesus is faithful to forgive us should cause you to always be full of His joy. The joy of forgiveness is full of peace and assurance that our God loves us eternally. Our names are written in the Lambs book of life, and we will be with the Lord forever. Knowing you're loved by the Lord, and forgiven, should always bring a smile to your face. You are never by yourself. The Lord is always with you.

Prayer:

Lord, I thank you for my salvation. I bless you for your amazing sacrifice you paid for my sins so I can be eternally forgiven. I love that I will be with you forever. Lord, I give you praise and glory that I am your child. Let me always be full of excitement and your joy for being in

Marcus L. Boston

the Your Kingdom. Thank you that I will spend eternity with you. In Jesus name. Amen.

Now spend time in praise and worship.

-Day 2-

Joy In God's Presence

Psalm 16 verse 11, "Thou wilt show me the path of light: in thy presence is fullness of joy; at thy right hand there are pleasures for evermore."

The biggest difference between the Old Testament and the New Testament is the Holy Ghost/Holy Spirit. In the Old Testament, they were not filled with the Spirit of God as we are today. Being born again in Christ Jesus is a greater experience for us today than they experienced in the Old Testament. They experienced the presence of God, and was enveloped in His pure joy, but not like us today. We are filled with the Spirit of God, and He lives inside of our spirit. He dwells in us.

Galatians chapter 5 verse 22 & 23, "But the fruit of the Spirit is love, joy, peace, long-suffering, gentleness, goodness, faith, meekness, temperance, against such there is no law." This fruit is from the Holy Spirit inside of us. Joy is inside of us within the Spirit of God inside of our spirit. Joy dwells inside of us.

The day I was filled with the Holy Ghost was an incredible encounter for me. When I first accepted Christ, I was not filled with the Holy Spirit immediately. Honestly, it took me several years before I was filled. I had a "closed spirit" because of the things I experienced in life. This is the equivalent of having walls up. We must freely allow the Holy Ghost within us. Here's how I was filled with the Holy Ghost.

"In the summer of 1996, on a Thursday, I was praising God with the fruit of my lips as I washed my dishes. I was telling the Lord how good He was when I suddenly felt something I never felt before. I knew it was the presence of God. I can't explain how I knew it was the Lord, but I knew it was Him. When He entered my kitchen, I became silent as I felt tingles all over my body. That's when I heard His voice softly say to me, "Let me in." I was hysterical and kept saying repeatedly, "OH, COME ON IN LORD, COME ON IN LORD!..." The Lord then said softly, "Shhhhh. Let me in." Again, I said loudly the same words and God repeated, "Shhhhh. Let me in." After taking a deep breath and calming myself down, I humbly replied, "God..., I don't know how to let you in, but will you help me let you in?" I felt the Lord and myself together open my spirit and God filled me with the Holy Ghost. I began to speak in tongues for the first time ever in my life. What an awesome experience I had with the Lord that evening. Since that day, I had beautiful communion with the Lord. I started praising the Lord longer and studying my bible longer. Eventually, I spent so much time with God that my television stayed off. I turned off the ringer on my phone. I didn't want to be disturbed when I spent time with the Lord. Sometimes I worshipped and praised my savior for hours. These hours seemed like a few minutes. I was enjoying my time with the Lord and it was so much better than when I wasn't filled with God's Spirit."

– A Pastor's Mistake page 16 & 17.

I shared this for those of you who have not been filled with the Holy Spirit. I know there's lots of teaching out there saying you are filled the day you receive Jesus as your savior. Well, that's not my testimony. I'm sure there are plenty of people out there who are being told they have God's Spirit, but they know He's not inside of them just yet. When God comes inside of you, you will definitely know it. No one will have to convince you or assure you He's inside of you. I was so full of joy after being filled with the Holy Ghost and speaking in tongues. I now have the double portion of God's joy. I have Him inside of me and I enjoy His presence outside of me. In the Old Testament, they only experienced God's presence outside of them. In the book of Acts chapter 19 verse 2, the question is asked, "Have ye received the Holy Ghost since ye believed?" These believers had never ever heard of the Holy Spirit. Regardless of what Christians are telling you, you have to know for yourself that you are filled for yourself. If you need to ask God, "Will you help me let you in?" So be it. And another thing, do not let anyone teach you to speak in tongues. The word of God says, "And they were all filled with the Holy Ghost, and began to speak with other tongues, as the Spirit gave them utterance." Act chapter 2 verse 4. I know some ministries that teach people to speak in tongues. If you were taught to speak in tongues, you need to ask God to purge you of false tongues. If the Holy Ghost is not speaking from within you, it's not the Holy Ghost. The Holy Spirit gave me my utterance. No one had to teach me anything. There are false tongues. Witches speak in false tongues and other satanic people. There are benefits to being filled with the Holy Ghost that can't be given by being taught to speak in tongues. Jude verse 20, "But ye, beloved, building up yourselves on your most holy faith, praying in the Holy Ghost." You can't pray in the Holy Ghost if you're not filled with the Holy Ghost. Those taught tongues have no power. "For he that speaketh in an unknown tongue speaketh not unto men; but unto God: for no man understandeth him; howbeit in the spirit he speaketh mysteries." "He that speaketh in an unknown tongue edifieth himself;." 1st Corinthians chapter 14 verse 2 & 4. You are speaking directly to God through the Holy Spirit and edifying yourself. You are building up yourself when you pray in the Holy Ghost. Who are you speaking to with your taught tongues? It's certainly not God and you're not building up yourself either. Please stop speaking in your taught false tongues.

My tongues have changed through the years. I do not speak in the same tongue I had when I was first filled. It keeps changing as the Holy Spirit gives me utterance. What spirit did you receive through fake tongues? To the people teaching tongues, what spirit is using you to do this? Nowhere in the bible does anyone teach tongues. Every church teaching tongues, repent and stop it.

There's a great joy that I carry because I know that God is inside of me and I know that I am His son. Regardless of the things I've experienced, you cannot tell me I'm not His child. I'm so happy that I've overcame so much church hurt to still be standing today. Study God's word and know His word for yourself. No matter what happens in our lives, we belong to God and He lives inside of us. We should always have joy because of this knowledge and understanding. Give God praise and worship, and enjoy your special moments with Him. I personally love when the Lord's presence comes upon me when I'm busy with life. I love when He comes upon me when I'm working or watching a movie. It's so wonderful being a child of the King. I joy in this all the time. In His presence is the fullness of joy, and Psalm Chapter 22 verse 3 says that God inhabits our praise to Him. So the Lord is inside of us and He dwells in our praises to Him. When you open your mouth and praise Him, when you dance and leap before Him, and when you cry out in love because of who He is, our God dwells inside of it. Hallelujah!!! Glory to God!!! Jesus is wonderful!!! Jesus is so amazing!!! I'm crying even as I write this to you. I'm giving Him the glory he deserves right now. Sweet Jesus!!! He dwells in our praise and He dwells inside of us. I know you have to be smiling and feeling grateful right now. This joy is peaceful. This joy is full of confidence that we belong to Jesus for eternity.

I really love corporate praise and worship. When we all come together with God inside of us and His presence fills the atmosphere surrounding us all at the same time is remarkable. We are so blessed to be in the Lord and we should rejoice over this understanding every day. We should always walk in the joy of God's presence every day. Amen.

Prayer:

Lord, I thank you for filling me with your precious Holy Spirit and that your joy lives inside of me. Help me to always do things that will cultivate the fruit of your Spirit within me. Help me seek your face, help me to praise and worship you daily. I bless you Lord and I ask you these things in Jesus name I pray. Amen.

(If you're not filled with the Holy Spirit, ask God to help you open up and receive His Spirit.)

-*Day 3*-

Joy In Rejection

"Blessed are ye, when men shall hate you, and when they shall separate you from their company, and shall reproach you, and cast out your name as evil, for the Son of man's sake. Rejoice ye in that day, and leap for joy; for, behold, your reward is great in heaven: for in the like manner did their fathers unto the prophets." Luke chapter 6 verse 22 & 23

If you've been a Christian for many years, I'm very sure you've experienced rejection by the saints of God. I've experienced this too many times and every time it seemed unbelievable. These things are written in the bible because these situations are going to occur. It's going to happen to you at some point by the people you love and fellowship with the most. It's very painful when it's members of your church. It's even more painful when you are rejected by people in the church leadership; especially if it's your pastor.

No matter how you are/were rejected, Jesus says to leap for joy. We have a great reward waiting for us in heaven, although I'm very sure we wish we could be rewarded right here on earth. Cry your tears and cast your cares unto the Lord. Try not to mediate on what happened. Keep casting it unto the Lord until you are healed and set free of the experience. Keep praying until you know you're free. Forgive them and let it go. I know, easier said than done. Well, I've experienced many rejections in the church and my name has been cast out as evil. I've been lied on by ministers, pastors, and prophets. People believe what they said because of their title and reputation. It really would be nice if believers had discernment to recognize they are being lied to. But hey, it is what it is. Nonetheless, I had to cast my cares on the Lord and forgive them. I had to let it go and move on with my life. I got to a place where I didn't care what they had to say about me anymore. You must also get to this place. You know what? When you experience this, it's like it just doesn't make any sense at all. It's so full of confusion and the bible says that God is not the author of confusion. You would think believers would try to stop the gossiping and strife. Nope, they become a vessel to spread it around freely. "Have you heard about such an such?" "Omg! Guess what such and such did?" I can't wait to tell you what such an such..." It's so clear in the word of God not to do these things, but tongue talking people participate anyway. Be encouraged by remembering day two. God is inside of you and He will never leave you nor forsake you. Do not be moved by the rejection of men, and do not leave Jesus because of them. Jesus loves you and always will. It is very painful, but if you keep seeking the Lord, you will heal and overcome it. Leap for joy, or should I say, jump towards heaven knowing

God is our very present help in the time of trouble, and in dealing with rejection. The joy in rejection is knowing that God will heal you and cause you to become a stronger more caring person after you're made whole.

Prayer:

Lord, I ask you to heal my broken heart over rejection. I cast all of my cares on you because you care for me. I forgive (call their names out) for rejecting me and I thank you God that you're going to heal me over this heartache. As I wait for you my healing, I will rejoice knowing you are my help. I bless you Lord and thank you. In Jesus name. Amen.

Now spend time in praise and worship.

(If you're guilty of rejecting and gossiping against members of the body of Christ, repent, and ask for forgiveness. Please stop it.)

-Day 4-

Joy In God's Promises

"For all the promises of God in him are yea, and in him Amen, unto the glory of God by us." 2nd Corinthians chapter 1 verse 20.

One thing that is extremely important for all of us as Christians is to learn the promises of our Heavenly Father. His promises are mentioned and written throughout the bible. One of the most popular chapters that include the promises/blessings of God is Deuteronomy chapter 28. However, on the other hand, it also reveals things that will happen if we are disobedient. Please remember these verses were written before the blood of Jesus was shed for all of our sins. In the Old Testament, we could not enter into the Holy of holies into the presence of God. God only allowed the high priest to come into His "pure" presence. If we entered the Holy of holies, we would drop dead instantly. The Lord's presence was on His terms in the Old Testament. 2nd Samuel chapter 6, verse 6 and 7, God killed Uzzah for touching the Ark Of The Covenant. Now we can go boldly before the throne of grace, covered in the blood of Jesus, and we can enter into the presence of God without restrictions and conditions like the high priest. We can confess our sins unto the Lord without bringing animals to the Levites to be sacrificed for our transgressions.

I'm not going to list any of the promises of God. Seek the Lord and find them throughout His word for yourself. One promise you should always keep in mind is that you will spend all eternity with Jesus because you received salvation. Salvation has many promises. Study the New Testament and learn them all. Take joy in these promises. They are all yours. What God has done for someone else, He will do it for you. There's a verse that says we overcome by the word of our testimony. It's important to share your testimonies with other believers, and to hear their testimonies. By doing this we encourage each other and build each other up. God has no respect of persons. He is faithful to us all. Take Jesus yoke upon you and learn of Him. Study the gospels and take joy in the promises Jesus spells out for you. It's so beautiful and wonderful to be with Jesus through salvation. Let's always rejoice in the Lord for being with Him. Amen? Amen.

Prayer:

Lord, I am so happy because your promises are guaranteed in my life. I thank you for all that you have for me in this lifetime, and in eternity. Help me to always be mindful of what you're going to do in my life, and help me to consistently rejoice over it all. In Jesus name. Amen.

Now spend time in praise and worship.

-Day 5-

Joy In Grieving

5 is the number of grace. Truly we all need the grace of God, especially when we are grieving over someone we love passing. I've been in this place several times. We all know that we will not live forever in our physical body, but that doesn't make it any easier.

"A merry heart doeth good like a medicine: but a broken spirit drieth the bones."
Proverb chapter 17 verse 22

After I received Jesus as my Lord and savior, I didn't experience death in my family until 8 years later. The interesting thing about this situation is that I felt death, or should I say I discerned death in my family. I prayed for my entire family. I called out everyone's names on my dad and mom's side of the family. I prayed for hours. The next day I prayed again for my entire family. Once again, I prayed for hours and called out everyone's name on both sides of my family. The following day I didn't feel death. I had a spirit of peace and believed the Lord heard me. The next day, which was a Saturday, my sister Vera passed. I shared this in my book, "A Pastor's Mistake." I was devastated! Most of all, I was angry at God! Here's what I wrote in my book.

"When I returned home, to my surprise, Kathy was sitting in the living room. I said hey and gave her a kiss. I had such a great time that day and I was not about to let anything spoil my evening. As I took my shower I asked the Lord to help me get sexually focused, so I could not only have sex with my wife, but also please her and be pleased too. I could tell something was on Kathy's mind. After showering, I sat on the sectional with my wife and asked, "I can see you have something to tell me. Well, what is it that you have to say?" Kathy took a slight breath and with a straight face uttered, "Your sister Vera died." I immediately put both of my hands on my head and ran to pray before the Lord. Even before I started praying, the tears poured from my eyes and I stretched out praying and crying to the Lord in anger."

-A Pastor's Mistake page 195

When you're angry at God, you might say some things that would have caused God to instantly kill you in the Old Testament. Thank God for the blood of Jesus. Even with the blood of Jesus, when you're angry at God, you must be careful not to blaspheme the Holy Ghost. "Wherefore, I say unto you, All manner of sin and blasphemy shall be forgiven unto men: but the blasphemy *against* the *Holy* Ghost shall not be forgiven unto men. And whosoever speaketh a word against the Son of man, it shall be forgiven him: but whosoever speaketh against the Holy Ghost, it shall not be forgiven him, neither in this world, neither in the *world* to come." Matthew chapter 12 verse 31 and 32.

Even though you may be angry, speak to the Lord with reverence, honor, and respect. Don't say anything you will regret. As you just read, there is one sin that will not be forgiven. Honestly, I do not fully understand why there is a sin that will not be forgiven. Be respectful if you're angry at God. The Lord did come speak to me about my sister Vera while I was crying to him in anger. I told God the truth in my heart. I was quoting His word to Him. Vera was the youngest of my 3 sisters. I'm that youngest of 4 children. She and I were close. When I visited Chicago from Tampa, she always had scheduled plans for us every time. This was too painful for me when she passed. She was 38 years old and I was 30. I felt like the Lord let me down. I felt as if God wasn't faithful to His word. There are things that happen in our lives with the Lord, we may never understand or receive answers concerning. One thing is certain, our faith and belief in God's word will be tested. I'm not saying God is testing us, but the things that happen in our lives will show us just how much we believe and trust the word of God.

When we are grieving, we must release the pain. It's ok to cry. Crying is releasing. Grieving can break our spirit. As you read at the beginning of this chapter, a broken spirit can dry the bones. What is this saying exactly? Well, our bones are extremely important. I suppose many have never considered where blood is created in our bodies. Blood is created in our bones. It's important to have a healthy grieving process. Have you ever noticed how some people get sick after someone they love dies? Their spirit is broken.

Spirit:

The part of a human associated with the mind, will, and feelings:

The essential nature of a person or group. Quality.

A person as characterized by a stated

quality.

An attitude marked by enthusiasm.

A mood or emotional state:

Strong loyalty or dedication.

The word spirit has many definitions. I only used the ones associated with this verse of scripture. When our mind, will, feelings, loyalty, dedication, mood and emotional state is broken by grieving, we must have a healthy grieving experience. It's ok to cry because you're going to miss them. It's ok to talk about the good times you've shared and precious memories you experienced with them. In the book of Deuteronomy chapter 34 verse 8, you'll read where the children of Israel wept because Moses was dead. It says they mourned (grieved) for 30 days. As Joshua took over leading the children of Israel, they moved on after the death of Moses and went into the promise land. I shared this to say that you must have a healthy grieving season. If you need counseling, please get some help. If you have people around you trying to help you you're blessed. There are people grieving who must go through it alone. Think on all of the good times and good memories that should bring a smile to your face. Remember, a merry heart does good like a medicine. Those small laughs from good memories will help you. These good memories will help your spirit to be recharged. The good you're remembering will help you heal. As much as you can, celebrate them in your own way, and do not neglect your life. You must still be there for your family, your children, your business, etc. Life goes on during the grieving process. Do not lose yourself.

I'm going to share 2 situations that actually happened. The first one is a man who lost his wife. He was happily married and his wife's passing destroyed his functionality in life. He was at the grave site every day and didn't want to leave. He would spend the entire day there every day. This man rose up on Mother's Day

The Joy *of the* Lord

and prepared breakfast for his wife who passed. He was so used to doing this every year that he did it unconsciously. It didn't hit him until he entered the bedroom saying, "Happy Mother's Day Baby. I love you.", but the bed was empty. He broke down and cried bitterly. On another occasion he was taking a shower and forgot his towel. He called out to his wife, "Baby, can you bring me a towel?", and then it hit him after he kept calling for her. Once again, he broke down and cried bitterly. My heart really went out to this man who called me for prayer. I prayed with him and kept him in my prayers. I checked on him consistently.

There's a woman who lost both of her parents a few months apart. She called me crying and shared everything in her heart. She began questioning God's word because God didn't heal them. She was praying for God to heal them and quoted many scriptures in faith. As she cried to me, I prayed quietly to myself, "God, please give me something to tell her. I need a word from you for her. Lord please..." I kept praying as she shared her heart and experience with me. Finally, the Holy Spirit gave me what to say. I gave her the following verse of scripture: Hebrews chapter 11 verse 13. "These all died in faith, not having received the promises, but having seen them afar off, and were persuaded of them, and embraced them, and confessed that they were strangers and pilgrims on the earth." How God gave it to me and how the Lord had me express what He was saying to her, caused her to rejoice as she cried tears of encouragement. God's presence was on our phone call and His compassion was intensely moving as I gave her what the Lord was saying. Sometimes we can have faith and not see the manifestation. It's better to die in faith than to die without it. Jesus did say in Luke chapter 18 verse 8, "Nevertheless, when the Son of man cometh, shall he find faith on the earth?"

Grieving in the Lord should be done with

prayers and seeking the Lord. If you do not have anyone physically there to help you grieve, you definitely have the Lord who is a very present help in the time of trouble. Psalm 46 verse 1. I hope you're not angry at God. I do understand though. As much as you can, think on good things and remember the good memories. Philippians chapter 4 verse 8. Jesus said in John chapter 14 verse 18, "I will not leave you comfortless: I will come to you." Many times while I was grieving and crying, the presence of God came to me and rested on me. Truly the Lord is a comforter and I love when God comes when I'm not calling on Him or praying. The joy in grieving is knowing God is a healer and a comforter. After my sister Vera passed, my father's mother passed, my father passed in 2005, and I've had many other family members pass as well since then. My oldest sister Deborah passed in 2021 to cancer. I'm still hurting over her. She was a pillar in our family. I miss her so much, but I am going on with my life. It's best to go forward with your life as you grieve. Do not let life go on without you and you're standing stagnant in grief. Do not lose yourself. Get professional counseling if you need it.

Prayer:

Lord, I ask you to heal me over the loss of (say their name or names). Help me to cherish their memory and celebrate their life (or lives). I need your comforting presence as I grieve Lord. Dry up all of my tears Lord and help me always smile over the good times I've shared with them. Strengthen me daily and help me move forward with my life. In Jesus name I pray. Amen.

(If the family is devastated. Add your family, children, friends, etc., to this prayer.)

-*Day 6*-

Joy In Hope

Proverbs chapter 13 verse 12, "Hope deferred maketh the heart sick, but when the desire cometh, it is a tree of life."

<u>Hope</u>:

To wish for a particular event that one considers possible:

To have confidence; trust.

To desire and consider possible:

The longing or desire for something accompanied by the belief in the possibility of its occurrence:

A source of or reason for such longing or desire:

The theological virtue defined as the desire and search for a future good, difficult but not impossible to attain with God's help.

Amen for these definitions.

defer:

To put off; postpone.

To delay or cause to be delayed until a future time; postpone.

To put off until a later time.

Losing hope is why many people commit suicide. A hopeless life is a life filled with depression and heaviness. No goals. No ambitions. An empty existence one has without hope. That feeling of emptiness causes people to stop valuing their own lives and death begins to look favorable. They believe nothing will ever improve. If you have no hope that things will get better, your will (spirit) to go on in life will be broken. As Christians our hope is very important. Our hope is connected directly to our faith. "Now faith is the substance of things hoped for, the evidence of things not seen." Hebrews chapter 11 verse 1. Faith is also a fruit of the Holy Spirit. In order for a Christian to lose hope, especially with all of the promises of God for us in this lifetime and in eternity written in the bible, many factors must take place.

I've seen it before, and some of you have as well, when Christians leave God. I left the Lord before. When this happened to me the first time, I was ignorant of the grace of God. I had a lack of knowledge of God's forgiveness. I had no idea how much God really loved me. I listened to the Christians around me who said I lost my salvation, and the most critical thing they said was God doesn't love me anymore. I left the church and hated Christians everywhere because of this experience in one church. I was backslidden. I was clueless and lost. This is when I began to have suicidal thoughts. The thought of God not loving me...; can you imagine how I felt? I had no understanding that God is married to the backslider.

Jeremiah chapter 3 verses 14 & 15,

"Turn, O backsliding children, saith the Lord;

For I am married unto you: and I will take you one of a city, and two of a family, and I will bring you to Zion: And I will give you pastors according to mine heart, which shall feed you with knowledge and understanding." Even you if you leave God, He is still connected to you. He's married to backsliders. So many of us have left the Lord because things that happened to us in the church, or what we have experienced in life. I shared how I became backslidden and how God brought me back to Himself in my book, "A Pastor's Mistake." I love the prophetic revelation that's in verse 15. Remember, this is the Old Testament and there were no pastors or churches. The church didn't begin until the book of Acts after Jesus' death and resurrection. Nice huh? Anyway, God is married to us even if we leave Him showing that His love is eternal and that truly He is faithful to forgive us.

The second time I was backslidden, I didn't realize that I was actually backslidden until I returned to church. I was fed up with many things and overwhelmed so much so that I told God, " "Lord, I'm tired of the church! I need a break from the church!" and I stopped going to church altogether. I wanted to be away from all church folks." "

From Woman To Woman

Volume Two page 235

I shared this entire experience in my books, "A Pastor's Mistake" and in my tell-all series, "From Woman To Woman Volume Two." The tell-all series is not for anyone under the age of 18. Reader discretion is advised for my tell-all books. Jesus is in all 3 books, although it may not appear that He's in there.

Always remember Proverbs chapter 14 verse 32, "...but the righteous hath hope in his death." We have promises in death and therefore we should have hope in this life. Never let go of your hope. Romans chapter 12 verse 11 says, "Rejoicing in hope; patient in tribulation; continuing instant in prayer." Be full of joy that you have hope. Rejoice! Be patient with the things you deal with in this life, and continue to be prayerful about everything. Hope is life. If you know someone backslidden, share this information with them so they can return to the Lord. Be encouraged and be full of hope in the Lord.

Prayer:

Lord, I pray that I never lose hope in you ever again. I pray that my hope increases and become strong faith in your promises in my life. I bless you Lord that you are married to me, and I am yours. Thank you for this amazing relationship I have with you. Help me rejoice in hope and let me forever grow in your grace with the things that I have to deal with in this life. In Jesus name. Amen.

Now spend time in praise and worship.

-*Day 7*-

Joy In Affliction

"For which cause we faint not; but though our outward man perish, yet the inward man is renewed day by day. For our light affliction, which is but for a moment, worketh for us a far more exceeding and eternal weight of glory;" 2nd Corinthians chapter 4 verses 16 and 17.

Affliction is nothing we desire to experience. Who loves pain? Who loves things that make you sad or sorrowful? Affliction doesn't feel good. In the book of Acts chapter 5 verse 41, the apostles rejoiced that they were counted worthy to suffer shame for Jesus' name. If you read the verses prior to this one, you will read they were also beaten. Why did they rejoice? They rejoiced because they knew Jesus personally. You must grow in your relationship with God. There are levels in the Lord. Jesus does not have respect of persons, but it's your responsibility to spend time with Christ. It's your responsibility to study your bible, spend time in prayer, and spend time giving the Lord praise and worship. Let's say you and someone both give your life to the Lord at the same time. One of you only goes to church, and the other goes to church, but takes time to read their bible, pray, and praise the Lord daily. Jesus loves you both, but the one that's spending time seeking the Lord will grow faster than you. I've seen this so many times when a person who's been going to church 30 years, but doesn't seek the Lord, tells someone who has only been in the church 5 years, "I know the Lord. There's nothing you can tell me." However, that person's 5 years was spent in prayer, reading the bible, and in praise and worship. The 30 years doesn't mean anything if you've never took time to get to know the Lord. There are many religious people in the church who do not spend time with God. Please seek the Lord and get to know Him.

Believing in Jesus is one thing. To know Jesus is another. The person who knows Jesus has a stronger walk than the person who only believes in Jesus. Jesus said, "Take my yoke upon you, and learn of me." Matthew chapter 11 verse 29. Growth is very important. Please seek the Lord. When afflictions come you will want to understand why, and knowing Christ will help you endure. "Herein is my Father glorified, that ye bear much fruit; so shall ye be my disciples." John chapter 15 verse 8. No growth equals no fruit. Jesus desires us to know Him, and we can't know Him if we do not spend time in the bible, prayer, and praise & worship.

"All the days of the afflicted are evil: but he that is of a merry heart hath a continual feast." Proverbs chapter 15 verse 15.

Affliction:

A condition of pain, suffering, or distress:

A cause of pain, suffering, or distress.

Something responsible for physical or

mental suffering, such as disease.

A distressed or painful state: misery.

A cause of mental or bodily pain.

A state of great suffering and distress due to adversity.

A condition of suffering or distress due to ill health.

I love how the bible is clear and doesn't sugarcoat affliction. It's evil. None of us desire any of these definitions, however, many of us; if not all of us, will experience affliction in some fashion. At the beginning of this chapter, we read where our affliction in this life is called light. Apostle Paul was saying this is nothing to faint about. We won't leave Jesus. We won't give up and go back to the world; which is going back to being with the devil. Yes, God is married to us, but if we refuse and rebel against Him because we don't like our life, that's a big problem. Isaiah chapter 1 verse 20. It's one thing if you're backslidden, but really desire to be with the Lord. It's another if you leave Him because you're angry at the things happening in your life.

Apostle Paul said though our outward man perish, our inward man is renewed day by day. We are renewed day by day because of our relationship with Christ. Studying our bible. Prayer. Praise and worship. Healthy fellowship with other Christians. All of these things helps us to be renewed every day because we know God is a very present help in the time of trouble. Our God is able to heal us. Our God is able to cause us to recover from affliction. These afflictions work for us because they cause us to run to Jesus. Our result is an eternal weight of glory in our Lord.

The apostles in Acts were able to rejoice in their afflictions because they knew the Lord personally. The world hates Jesus and they hate us; especially these days. Regardless of the things that happen to us, we are in Christ and if affliction comes into our lives, God will work it out for our good. Romans chapter 8 verse 28. When you know and understand that Christ is with you in affliction, you can rejoice like the apostles. "He that is of a merry heart has a continual feast." You can have a continual feast of joy in affliction. "Looking unto Jesus the author and finisher of our faith; who for the joy that was set before him endured the cross, despising the shame, and is set down at the right hand of the throne of God." How could the cross be joy to Jesus? The joy of seeing many souls being eternally saved through His sacrifice for our sins. We can have this same joy in our affliction knowing it's working for us an eternal weight of His glory. I'm not saying it's going to be a piece of cake, but our hearts can take joy in knowing the Lord will work it out for us. We can have a continual feast that is renewed every day in our affliction by Jesus. Every day new strength and joy. Be patient, be encouraged, be full of hope, and seek the Lord. Amen.

Prayer:

Lord, help me to have a continual feast of your joy when I experience affliction in my life. You are with me and because of this, I have confidence in you. I can rest, have peace, and rejoice in you because you are my comfort and strength. Help me to seek your face daily so I can be renewed in your power day by day. I bless your wonderful name. I give you glory. In Jesus name. Amen.

-*Day 8*-

A Joyful Heart

"A good man out of the good treasure of his heart bringeth forth that which is good; and an evil man out of the evil treasure of his heart bringeth forth that which is evil: for of the abundance of the heart his mouth speaketh." Luke chapter 6 verse 45.

Most of us will probably say, "I have a good heart." Most people who are in the world, and who don't know God will say, "I have a good heart." When I was out in the world going "From Woman To Woman," I still said, "I have a good heart." Sin blinds us from seeing ourselves clearly. We may have some good qualities in our heart, but we fail to identify or purposely overlook the evil things. Some of us even justify ourselves by saying, "Well, at least I've never did ...." We compare ourselves to others to make us feel better about ourselves personally. When I was first saved, I believed all I had to do was stop fornicating and I would be a perfect person. I was so full of pride and very arrogant that I couldn't see myself. I believed I was a good person. God saved me because I was a good person. This is why so many people who have killed people feel as if they can't be saved. Jesus died for murderers, child molesters, and he also died for the sex traffickers. Jeffrey Dahmer, who killed and ate his victims, gave his life to Jesus before he was killed in prison. Internet search "Jeffrey Dahmer becomes a Christian." A prison minister led him to Christ and baptized him. I know so many people desire these people to go to hell, but if they come to Jesus sincerely and give their lives to Him, Jesus receives them. Yes, Jesus receives them. Killers on death row can be saved. Drug dealers, gang bangers, drug cartels, and corrupt politicians can be saved. Those neighborhood thots, sluts, and whores with all those children with multiple fathers can be saved. Porn stars, prostitutes, homosexuals, and everyone else can be saved. Everyone can come to Jesus, even if you don't want them too. I can't stand the Christians who turn their noses up at people who come to church dressed in ways they don't approve of. Stop it! Show them the love of Christ. It happened to me and I understand. We need our hearts purified.

How do you know you have a good heart? "The heart is deceitful above all things, and desperately wicked: who can know it? I the Lord search the heart, try the reins, even to give every man according to his ways, and according to the fruit of his doings." Thank God for the blood of Jesus. I'm so glad God didn't give us what we really deserved. After King David was rebuked, corrected, and exposed by Prophet Nathan, 2nd Samuel chapter 12, David humbled himself. This is when David wrote Psalm 51. Please read it right now.

King David knew that his heart wasn't pure.

He asked the Lord, "Create in me a clean heart, O God; and renew a right spirit within me." I love when David said, "Restore unto me the joy of thy salvation;" Being guilty of sin is painful. Failing God should hurt. Fortunately for us, there is no condemnation to those who are in Christ. Roman chapter 8 verse 1. David needed his joy back. David had sex with a married woman, got her pregnant, tried to get her husband to have sex with his wife so the husband would think the baby is his, and when that didn't work, David killed him; yet David had something in his heart that God loved. The word of God says David was a man after God's heart. 1st Samuel chapter 13 verse 14. God knows our hearts. Moses was a murderer, but wrote the first 5 books of the bible. Apostle Paul was a murderer and Jesus appeared to him (Acts chapter 9), he wrote most of the New Testament, and we are Christians today because of his ministry. There are many people in the Bible who have committed evil, but God came into their lives and made a great change.

"For out of the heart proceed evil thoughts, murders, adulteries, fornications, thefts, false witness (liars), blasphemies:." Matthew chapter 15 verse 19. Ask God to create in you a clean heart, and renew the right spirit within you. Deliverance from evil fruit in our hearts causes joy to spring up. The joy of your salvation is good, but once you see God purging you, cleaning you, and washing you, your joy will increase. Remember, joy is the fruit of the Spirit. Think of a fruit tree. There's always more than just one piece of fruit on it. You can have multiple areas of joy in your life at the same time. This book is designed so you can have a life full of the Joy of the Lord.

You would be amazed at the things in your heart that you are unaware of. King David said, "Cleanse thou me from secret faults." Psalm 19 verse 12. I remember saying several times, "I would never do this." or "I would never do that." Well, I did those things eventually and afterwards, exactly what I said came back to my memory. I couldn't believe I did what I said I would never do. It was very humbling and sobering. Praying for a pure heart is a must for believers. Even as the bible says, lest a root of bitterness springs up, we don't want the wrong thing in our hearts springing up at the wrong time. As God sets you free and break chains in your life, you're going to start hearing people say, "You are glowing.", "You look so happy.", or something similar. I've experienced this and it's a beautiful thing.

"A merry heart maketh a cheerful countenance:" Proverbs chapter 15 verse 13

I've had people upset with me because of my joy, "Why are you always so happy? It's sickening! I hate that look on your face!" I didn't even realize I was so joyful. I was just living my life. I've heard this in different ways from different people over the years. I've also heard, "You brighten up my day every time I see you. I look forward to seeing your smile."

There are times in our walk with God when we are unaware of our personal growth. I believe these things happen so we can see we are making progress spiritually. "Let your light so shine before men, that they may see your good works, and glorify your Father which is in heaven." Matthew chapter 5 verse 16. Our works isn't just the good deeds we do, but we must work on ourselves. You can do many good works and still have no joy. There are many miserable Christians and I've known many through the years. They are sad, depressed, heavy, weighed down, and bound with oppression. It's almost like it's impossible to encourage them. If you're this type of Christian, I pray this book is the answer to your prayers. A heart full of joy is priceless.

Prayer:

Lord, I thank you that I am your child. Father, I yield all of my heart to you and I ask you to purify my heart. Wash my heart of all evil and impurities, and let my heart be full of good deeds, good works, and all things that will let my light shine in this world for your glory. Let my face shine with your joy and let people ask me why I am so happy so I can share the gospel with them. I bless you Lord. In Jesus name I pray. Amen.

-Day 9-

Joyful Conversations

I recall when I was first saved, I had joy for a season. I was so happy that I finally knew the truth about God. I was searching for God as a nonbeliever. When I say nonbeliever, I didn't believe the bible and I fought Christians at every opportunity. Once I understood the bible was the true and living God's word, and I gave my life to Him, I was joyful for a season. I came to church fresh out of the world and believed those who were already in the church were perfect people. I was very naïve and ignorant of the bible. I learned very quickly how ugly things in the church can be with fellow believers. I was so tired of being rebuked every week before church and my joy left me. I would sit in church looking angry and upset. I remember when someone said on the microphone during church, "Smile Brother

The Joy *of the* Lord

Marcus." I am glad those days are over.

"Out of the same mouth proceedeth blessing and cursing. My brethren, these things ought not so to be." James chapter 3 verse 10

The book of James, as well as other epistles in the New Testament, talks about how Christians use their mouths in the wrong manner. There were a group of us who got saved around the same time and we were all babes in the Lord. It's like we became the worst of enemies. My mouth kept me in trouble. I was in the pastor's office every week because of something I said to someone. I had no scriptures in my heart and no Holy Ghost. I was raw and straight forward. All I could do was be myself, however, there are people in our churches who know better and still use their mouths negatively. With death and life in the power of our tongues, and words being spirit and life, we should earnestly pursue to speak in healthy ways. Again, if our hearts were pure, we would have better character.

When your heart is being purged and purified toward the Lord, your mouth will change. You may not even notice it at first. When I began speaking joy, I didn't really understand how or why. As I got closer to God and experienced deliverance, healing, and growth in the word, my speech changed. Saints and coworkers began asking me, "What are you so happy about?" "Why are you so happy?" "Who got you smiling?" I received many of these questions over the years. The word says from the abundance of the heart, the mouth speaks. As your heart gets cleaner and you get closer to God, the joy in your spirit begins to enter your heart. It becomes one with you. You can know many things, but if it's not in your heart, is it a part of you? No. It's just knowledge. I really don't like when Christians say, "Fake it til you make it." I hate being fake. I was married and we both were faking like our marriage was good. I admit, married couples shouldn't go around looking like they are absolutely miserable, but there must be truth and honesty to a certain degree. This is why people are shocked when they hear married couples are getting divorced. "They looked so happy." This is the normal response because they were faking it and didn't make it. Listen, I will not live in a miserable marriage. I wrote the book, "For Better or Worse. Why Christians Get Divorced?" during our separation. God gave me a very powerful revelation on marriage and as he explained His revelation to me, I wrote a book about it. No details of my former marriage are within the book, despite so many people thinking I was attacking my ex-wife. This revelation changed how I see marriage. I can't live a lie; no, I won't live a lie. Life is too short to living a fake existence. I packed and left. I have no regrets. Best decision for my life.

Let your joy be true. Don't act like you're full of joy, be full of joy. Stay focused on the joy of being forgiven in your salvation as you seek to grow in grace. Don't be a fake in your Christian walk. "A man hath joy by the answer of his mouth: and a word spoken in due season, how good is it!? Proverbs chapter 15 verse 23 Telling jokes and having a heart full of joy are two different things. I would rather have a heart of joy instead of joking around. Jokes are funny, but there are people who tell jokes and are not happy. Comedians have committed suicide. It's so shocking to find out people who look happy are not really happy. Be happy in Christ.

Let the conversations you have be full of joy. Let every answer of your mouth be edifying, graceful, righteous, and encouraging. Let it be in your heart, from your heart, and let your words be wholesome. When people want to gossip, slander, and share negative things with you, please guard your heart and stop that conversation. I've experienced this several times. After hearing negative information about someone, whether it was true or lies, when I saw that person it's like I didn't want to talk to them. I wanted to avoid them and they did not do anything to me. I had to pray those things out of my heart. Seeds of discord are real and God hates it. Monitor your words and the conversations you participate in. What you hear affects your heart. Be careful not to receive, "Seeds of discord." Proverbs chapter 6 verse 16 -19. "These six things doth the Lord hate, yea, seven are an abomination unto him: A proud look, a lying tongue, and hands that shed innocent blood, A heart that deviseth wicked imaginations, feet that be swift in running to mischief, a false witness that speaketh lies, and he that soweth discord among the brethren." God says seeds of discord are an abomination. Well, if you've been a Christian for many years, you already know how much this happens among believers. The Lord hates it, yet it happens too often through lies, gossip, slander, and judging one another. I'm sure you've experienced what I shared a little earlier about hearing negative information and then you find yourself having an issue with the person you heard the negative information about. Your heart is now full of seeds of discord. Hopefully, this has never happened to you. Stop allowing people with gossip etc., to fill your ears because what you hear leads to your heart. When they start talking negatively about someone or a situation, stop them and give them the word of God. "Blessed are the pure in heart, for they shall see God." Matthew chapter 5 verse 8

Keep your heart pure. Have conversations that will build up individuals, and not spread negative information. Let your mouth speak joy and love. Let the answers of your mouth reflect the condition of your heart. Gossipers and slanderers hearts are not pure. If you're a gossiper, please stop it. Ask God to purify your heart. "Let the words of my mouth, and the meditation of my heart, be acceptable in thy sight, O Lord, my strength, and my redeemer." Psalm 19 verse 14

"And whatsoever ye do in word or deed, do all in the name of the Lord Jesus, giving thanks to God and the Father by him."

Colossians chapter 3 verse 17

Prayer:

Lord, I yield my mouth and tongue to you for your glory. I repent for everyone I've talked about and I ask you to forgive me. Forgive me for spreading negative information and planting seeds of discord. I ask you to purify my heart of all gossip, and slander. Help me to use my mouth to edify and build up others for good. Let the answer of my mouth be full of your joy, unity, and peace. Let me not be a tool of negativity, but a tool that gives you glory and honor. Help me speak words that are in due season and good! Help me not to listen to negative information, slander, and gossip. When anyone comes to me with gossip, help me to stop them, and give them the word of God. I bless your wonderful name. In Jesus name I pray. Amen.

-Day 10-

Joy In Peace

"Blessed are the peacemakers: for they shall be called the children of God."
Matthew chapter 5 verse 9

Isn't it amazing how many things we hear preached these days. We really don't hear many messages or sermons on peacemakers. We hear about prosperity more than we hear about being peace makers. We hear more about giving and sowing money more than being a peacemaker. Jesus said blessed are the peacemakers for they shall be called the children of God. Well, there's more to what Jesus was about being a peacemaker. In the book of Isaiah chapter 28 verse 10, the scripture is talking about how the word of God connects with itself. Line upon line (verse upon verse) and here a little & there a little (book connecting to book). The verse I'm about to give you, I have never heard preached ever by anyone.

"but to the counselors of peace is joy." Proverbs 12 v 20

To all the counselors of peace, God will give you joy. There's a reward to the peacemakers. Jesus values peacemakers so much that He said they shall be called the children of God, and you also receive joy for your efforts. I admit, it takes a special quality to be a peacemaker. What is this quality? Is it love? Is it compassion? It's both. It also takes energy to help people work through their issues. Not everyone desires to do this. Isn't it amazing how many people record drama and post it? We rarely see anyone trying to stop the people from fighting or arguing. Peacemakers are a beautiful people.

Counselor has many definitions. The only one I like for what we are talking about is "Adviser." The president of the United States is surrounded by advisers. Most leaders of nations around the word have advisers. Wouldn't it be incredible if all these advisers desired all nations to be at peace with other nations? Peacemakers are important. Be a peacemaker in your family, your church, and everywhere you abide. We shouldn't desire chaos, confusion, strife, backbiting, and other negative things to continue unchecked. There's power in unity and being on one accord. Imagine if everyone in every church actually had unity, and no one was at odds with each other. This would be an amazing event to behold. In addition, when we are one accord in our congregations, God can move in more powerful ways. If everyone came to church with a pure heart, we would see God move in extraordinary ways every service. However, many churches have people who keep the drama and foolishness circulating, which shows the condition of their heart.

Joy is given to the counselors of peace. Be a

peacemaker. More joy will be added to your life. For those of you who are already peacemakers, I already know you're nodding your head and smiling because you have this joy presently. You probably didn't know why keeping the peace makes you so happy. Well, now you know. Keep it up.

Prayer:

Lord, help me to be a peacemaker. Bless me with the knowledge and good quality to be an adviser to achieve peace. Help me have the love and compassion I need to be a peacemaker. Thank you that you will give me joy for being a counselor of peace. Let my heart be pure of everything that causes division and breaks unity. Let me not contribute to foolishness in my family, or church, but let me be the person who helps people overcome their issues with each other. In Jesus name. Amen.

Now spend time in praise and worship.

Marcus L. Boston

-Day 11-

Joy In Victory

I know this should be the easiest joy to have for most of us, however, there are some people who can't rejoice even when they win. Some of them have an inability to recognize victory because they have been through so much turmoil. They are so accustomed to losing and being disappointed that they expect it to continue in their life. "Casting all your care upon him; for he careth for you." 1st Peter chapter 5 verse 7. If you're experiencing this, please give all of your cares to the Lord in prayer. Do all you can to let it go unto the Lord. You must learn to pray and you must study as many scriptures on giving your burdens to God. "Come unto me, all ye that labor and are heavy laden, and I will give you rest." Matthew chapter 11 verse 28. Your rest and peace is in Jesus. Your healing is in Jesus. Seek Him and He will manifest Himself to you.

When Solomon was made king (1st king chapter 1), this was a great promotion for him. Verse 40 specifically says how they rejoiced with great joy. Psalm 75 verses 6 & 7 declares, "For promotion cometh neither from the east, nor from the west, nor from the south. But God is the judge: he putteth down one, and setteth up another." Whenever promotion comes, you should be full of joy because God did this for you, and this brings me to my next point.

You may be going through somethings that you hate or despise. Do not be a hater, jealous, or envious when God promotes someone around you. Do not feel bad because it's not you. "Rejoice with them that do rejoice," Romans chapter 12 verse 15. If you cannot celebrate someone else's victory, you should check your heart. Why can't you rejoice for them? Are they your enemy? If they are your enemy, would you celebrate if calamity hits their life? Would you be happy tragedy struck your enemy? I'm not going to bother quoting Jesus saying love your enemy. This verse is popular. How about I give you an unpopular verse?

"Rejoice not when thine enemy falleth, and let not thine heart be glad when he stumbleth: Lest the Lord see it, and it displease him, and he turn away his wrath from him."

Proverbs chapter 24 verses 17 & 18

See, this is why so many of our enemies will not reap what they have sown because our hearts desire to see the Lord destroy them. Loving your enemy allows God to do whatever it is He's going to do to reward or recompense evil done to us. Which is a sign of what? It's a sign that your heart is not pure. I pray for my enemies. I pray they repent and get it right with God. I already know they will reap what they have sown; this is guaranteed. Whether they are a Christian or not, they will reap what they have sown. I know it's not easy to forgive great evils done against us, but ask God to help you forgive them.

Give God the praise when He gives you victories and promotions. Always show Him how much you appreciate what He has done for you. Worship Him, Praise Him, and tell Him how much you love Him. This should be the easiest of all joy for many of us. Jump and leap for joy. Dance and celebrate. Throw a party. Go out to dinner. If you're not into those things, find something to do that give you joy and show forth the joy of your victory given by Jesus.

Prayer:

Lord, I thank you for victory in my life. Thank you that I'm going from glory to glory in you and I know more victories are to come. Help me celebrate those who have victory and promotion. Let me have genuine joy for what you've done in their lives. I cast all my cares on you as I wait for my next victory, and I rejoice because I know you're going to do for me. I pray that you bless my enemies and help them to seek your face. Help my enemies get to know you so they can be forgiven for their sins, and the things they did unto me. I praise your beautiful name Lord. I love you so much. I ask this prayer in your son's name Jesus. Amen.

Now give the Lord some victorious praise.

-*Day 12*-

Joy In Praise

God loves our praise. Whether you are giving God personal praise at home, or whether it's during corporate ministry services, God loves our praise. He comes and inhabits our praise. There are times when things in our life may not be favorable, and it could be difficult to give God praise. You could even be disappointed with God because of how things played out in your life. You could be under heavy spiritual attacks by the enemy. I've experienced many things that I had to press my way through. Giving up is not an option in my life. Giving up on God is the equivalent to saying, "I'm going back to be with the devil, and go to hell."

I've learned to praise God in the best and worst of situations. I believe most of us have not experienced what Job went through. Read the first few chapters of Job if you're not knowledgeable. Job chapter 1 verse 21 says Job praised God although he just experienced great tragedy. Verse 22 says, "In all this Job sinned not, nor charged God foolishly." I couldn't imagine being in Job's shoes. Job knew God very well to praise God and not blame Him for his calamities. Please seek the Lord and get to really know Him. You'll learn to praise Him because it's right and because He deserves it. I've learned to love giving God praise and I'm totally elated while I'm blessing Him.

Psalm 27 verse 6, "And now shall mine head be lifted up above mine enemies round about me: therefore will I offer in his tabernacle sacrifices of joy; I will sing, yea, I will sing praises unto the Lord." This entire Psalm will bless your soul. King David said he will offer sacrifices of joy in the toughest of situations. At my sister Vera's funeral, I gave a sacrifice of praise. I had never seen anyone giving God praise at a funeral before, and I'll share this experience with you. "The next morning was the funeral and I didn't look forward to it. Kathy's mom attended and that was comforting. As the order of the funeral went on, I held back my tears as much as I could. My family held up pretty well under the circumstances. But when the choir began to sing their second selection, "I Believe," the glory of God suddenly filled the place. Without a single thought, I jumped to my feet with my hands raised as high as they could go. Once I was up on my feet with my hands extended high, I thought, [What am I doing? This is a funeral.] Then I heard the voice of the Lord say, "Yield." As I yielded to the Spirit of God, I danced as the choir sang. At that moment I knew my sister's name was written in the Lamb's book of life and she was with the Lord. Whether she was sleeping and waiting for the trumpet to sound, or whether she was already in heaven present with the Lord, it didn't matter. Either way I knew she made it and I danced tearfully before the Lord. The glory of God saturated my sister's home going service. Wow! I have never been to a funeral where the glory of God filled the service. When it was over someone informed me that Kathy's mother was dancing too. This added more joy to my heart. I wished Kathy praised the Lord like her mother. The presence of God was at my sister's funeral and the Lord glorified her. The joy I had because of this was tremendous, and I couldn't wait to testify back in Tampa. We went back to Tampa that Monday. Once we were back at home, Kathy was a little nicer to me along with Pastor Davis."

A Pastor's Mistake pages 198 – 199

At the time this happened, I didn't see this as a sacrifice. God told me to yield because I was going to withhold praising Him. I'm glad He spoke to me and I'm glad I yielded. A sacrifice of joy will be a praise that you really don't want to give, a praise that will come during a very hard time in your life, or a praise that you will give just for one reason, and one reason only; God deserves it because He is God.

David talked about war rising up against him and being surrounded by his enemies in Psalm 27. David fought physical battles. Our battles these days are mostly spiritual. If you have the gift of discernment (1st Corinthians chapter 12), you have the ability to see, perceive, or feel when evil spirits are around you. You may even see evil spirits on someone. There are times when you may feel evil spirits attacking you or weighing you down because of a sin you may have committed. Then again, you may not have any of these within your gift. You may be able to discern when someone is lying or you may discern situations. This gift is not the same for all believers. I've talked with many believers and we all discerned the same type of thing differently. There are believers who don't believe in discernment and if that's you, ok. I'm not going to debate or argue with you. Remember this: your gifts function only as far as you believe. If you don't believe in miracles, you won't see any &

God will not use you to perform a miracle because of your unbelief. If you don't believe in prophecy, ok, that's you. However, you will not war a good warfare like Timothy was instructed. 1st Timothy chapter 1 verse 18. You limit yourself with unbelief and being faithless. By the way, for the prophecy unbelievers, "worship God: for the testimony of Jesus is the spirit of prophecy." Revelation chapter 19 verse 10. Jesus Christ is the same yesterday, today, and forever. Hebrews chapter 13 verse 8. For more on spiritual warfare and discernment, read my book "Enchanted." For all information on prophecy, read my book "Tainted Influence. Identifying Prophetic Truth & Error.

Learn to love giving God praise. If you learn to love God's presence, when He manifests His Spirit, your reaction will be like mine at my sister's funeral. My love for Him caused an immediate reaction of praise even though I was hurting and grieving. I've learned to praise God when I'm under heavy spiritual attacks and strong witchcraft attacks. You may not feel like it, but give a sacrifice of joy anyway. A joyful praise; not a sad defeated depressed praise. If that's the best you can do, do it until it becomes joy; a sacrifice of joy.

Prayer:

Lord, help me to not only give you praise, but help me to offer sacrifices of joy unto you no matter what is going on in my life. Let the fruit of my lips bless you in every situation and circumstance that comes my way. You never promised an easy life, but you promised to never leave me nor forsake me. In this let me celebrate your great name and bless you at all times. I adore you Lord. In Jesus name I pray. Amen.

Now spend time in praise and worship.

-*Day 13*-

Joy Over Your Enemies

This joy can be one of the most rewarding feelings ever. We all have enemies. An enemy is someone who is 100% against your life. We call them haters today. They do not desire you to make it at all. They do not celebrate when things go well for you. They pray evil prayers against your life. What's an evil prayer? Well, evil prayers come from believers with polluted hearts. If you're thinking, "Christians cannot pray evil prayers." You're wrong. If you're praying for God to destroy people's lives or kill them, these are evil prayers. In the Old Testament, you see plenty of these prayers because their enemy was a physical one. Jesus now says to love your enemy.

Once you gracefully love your enemy, you will see victory over your enemy. There is no time frame though, but this only happens when God decides it's time. Like you read previously, God will turn His wrath away from your enemies if you desire to see them destroyed. Now that Jesus has died and rose again for the salvation of all human souls, God doesn't desire to see anyone destroyed. "The Lord is not slack concerning his promise, as some men count slackness; but is long-suffering to us-ward, not willing that any should perish, but that all should come to repentance." 2nd Peter chapter 3 verse 9

Longsuffering is God being very patient with us. Why is the Lord so patient with us? Because Jesus died for our sins and all of our sins are forgiven when you receive Jesus as your savior. This patience is His grace. Even though we may not care for what our enemies have done to us, God still loves them. We may even hate them purely for the evils performed against us or our families; well, God still loves them. They will reap what they sowed, but we need to get our hearts purified toward our enemies.

"Then they returned, every man of Judah and Jerusalem, and Jehoshaphat in the forefront of them, to go again to Jerusalem with joy; for the Lord made them to rejoice over their enemies."

2nd Chronicles chapter 20 verse 27

Verse 29 says the Lord fought against the enemies of Israel. The rules have changed since then, but the Lord is the same who will fight for us. God will bless us to rejoice over our enemies. God will prepare a table before us in the presence of our enemies. (Psalm 23) Be patient. This day will come. Ask God to cleanse your heart and when victory comes, you will praise God with joy and liberty. I've seen enemies defeated by the hand of God. Some were Christian enemies. Yes, I have enemies who are Christians and when God gave me victory over them, I felt sorry for them. I wasn't happy God had to judge them. Several of these victories are recorded in my book, "A Pastor's Mistake." One of my enemies was my pastor and many others in that former church. It's a big book because it was a lot to write. I recorded our church services and quoted him verbatim in my book. I also shared my journal entries. You'll experience what I went through as if you were right there with me. I can safely say my ex-wife is my enemy. She's lying on me publicly. I was very angry and went before God about it. I called my attorney and was asking if I should take her to court for defamation of character. My attorney, who is a believer, told me, "We are going to let God handle her." Here's when I knew my heart was finally pure toward my ex-wife. I received a call saying my ex-wife said I was beating her. I didn't get mad, upset, or angry. I didn't bother praying about it. I went to sleep and the next day, God said, "You finally overcame (ex-wife name). Now you're ready to go where I'm taking you." In my book, "From Woman To Woman Volume Three," because of everything I endured with my ex-wife, I shared our story in truth. I wrote what really happened with us and why our marriage failed. It's a sad embarrassing story. I was relieved and at peace when I knew my heart was finally pure toward her. Listen, if you want victory over your enemies, forgive them and overcome the evils they did to you. Cast this care or cares to the Lord and move on. I did.

Prayer:

Lord, I ask you to wash me clean of everything my enemies have done to me. I forgive them and let it go. I ask you to save my enemies and lead them to repent to you. When you do give me victory over them, I pray I rejoice in You with all humbleness of heart and mind. I bless you as I wait to see your Hand move on my behalf. In Jesus name I pray. Amen

Now, spend some time sharing your heart in truth concerning your enemies. Let out all of your emotions and leave them with the Lord.

-*Day 14*-

Joy In Restoration

I took some time trying to find a bible verse for what I'm about to share. I mentioned earlier about when I was backslidden. Well, after the saints convinced me that God didn't love me anymore and that I lost my salvation, I left the church. How did I get back into the church? The Lord came Himself to restore my soul. Here's what I wrote in my book, "A Pastor's Mistake."

"In the month of November 1998, while alone in my apartment, I cried out to the Lord to come save me from my sins. I had been in a backslidden condition for almost two years and was dreadfully missing the presence of the Lord. Several hours passed by, as I cried watching Fred Hammond's live concert on VHS; six hours to be exact. I kept rewinding and listening to the videotape, over and over

---

repeatedly, as the tears flowed. Suddenly, I fell on my face sobbing and weeping as I felt the presence of God enter my living room. I realized immediately that the Lord heard my cry. While I was still on my face, my left hand started turning in a circular motion. I kept trying to stop my hand from turning, but to no avail. Then I heard the Lord say, "I'm wiping the slate clean." After the Lord had spoken those words, He began to purge me and afterwards, tears of appreciation began to fall rapidly. God was cleaning me and destroying those things that had me bound since I left the church in February 1997. God proved that He truly loved me and it felt so good to know that God heard me as I cried out for His hand of salvation." A Pastor's Mistake page 1

A clean slate is like you're starting over. A new beginning. After this encounter with God, I knew the Lord loved me. I experienced a sweet peaceful joy when the Lord restored me. The pastor didn't call me or come by my apartment when I stopped going to their church. What happened to restoring someone? What happened to leaving the 99 and looking for that lost sheep? Well, that's not my testimony.

Restoration can be different for all of us. What occurred in your life that you no longer have in God? In order to be restored, there has to be a place that you no longer occupy. It can be viewed as something lost or something being removed. It can be a demotion. You don't have to be backslidden to experience this. What is it that you desire to have again? What do you desire to be restored in your life? Marriage? Friendships? Positions? Your family? The voice of God? I feel like some of you will be crying during this chapter. What did you lose that you desire to be returned unto you? What happened that caused you to need restoration? Was it sin? A fight? A disagreement? Slander or lies? God is a restorer. Here's a verse that relates to what I'm saying.

"But many of the priests and Levites and

chief of the fathers, who were ancient men, that had seen the first house; when the foundation of this house was laid before their eyes, wept with a loud voice; and many shouted aloud for joy:" Ezra chapter 3 verse 12.

This chapter is focused on the rebuilding of the Lord's house. The first house that was built during King Solomon's time was destroyed. The old men which had seen the first house of the Lord, cried and shouted out loud with joy that the Lord's house was being rebuilt. It wasn't completed, but they celebrated once the foundation was finished. These men cried because the Lord's house was in the process of restoration. They had tremendous joy before seeing the finished product. They celebrated the progress.

This is how we should be when God brings or begins restoration in our lives. When God restored me from being backslidden, I was not healed from the hurt of what lead me to being backslidden or the things I did when I was backslidden. I share these things in my books, "A Pastor's Mistake" and "From Woman To Woman Volume Two." Nonetheless, I was full of joy because the slate was wiped clean, and a new beginning began for my life. Most of all, I was relieved that God does love me. Restoration is something we should all have joy concerning. I believe it was a wonderful sight to see those old men crying and shouting with joy because God's house was being restored. This noise of weeping and shouting for joy could not be discerned. (verse 13) There are many things in the bible I wished I could have witnessed. This event is one of them. If you have ever experienced restoration, I'm sure your joy was overflowing. I know my joy could not be measured. I've witnessed people receive restoration and their joy was a beautiful sight. If you're waiting on restoration, be patient, be hopeful, believe it will happen, and stand in faith until you experience it. God will do it for you.

Prayers:

Lord, I ask you to restore me. Everything that the enemy stole from me, I ask you to restore sevenfold. Help me be patient and help me never to doubt you will do this for me. I thank you in advance and I praise you for my restoration now. I give you glory, honor, and worship. In Jesus name. Amen.

Now spend time in praise and worship.

-*Day 15*-

Joy In Parenting

I love being a father and I loved the relationship I had with my very own father. My father passed in 2005 and it hit me very hard. It was completely unexpected, and I needed the Lord's strength and comfort to make it through that grieving process. The Lord kept reminding me of many great memories I shared and reminded me of many more I had long forgotten about. I didn't know our last conversation would be the last time I seen my father alive. Actually, it would be the last time I've seen him ever. I joy in the fact that I shared all of my heart with him. I shared how I desired us to go on a cruise together, how I desired us to take some professional pictures, and many more things. We talked for hours. In response to everything I shared, my father said several things that really made me feel better about myself. My father said, "Son, you're going to make it. You're a very smart young man. You have many ideas and something you do will work. You never give up and you keep trying to do new things. You'll make it son. I have no doubt about it." The only thing I didn't inform my father is that I was writing my first book. I wanted it to be a surprise. Twelve books later I really wished I told him.

I shared this with you because I never wanted to make my father feel ashamed I was his son. I did that once as a child when I failed the 6th grade. I didn't even try to pass. I was living with him and moved back in with my mom. I was placed in a new school and hated it. I suppose I lost myself and my motivation. I didn't do my homework and I didn't pay attention in class. I lied to my father when he asked me how I was doing in school. When I was told I had to repeat the 6th grade, this is when I saw the error of my ways. My father was very disappointed in me and I never wanted him to ever feel like this toward me ever again. Moreover, when I walked in the same classroom hearing those students whispering about me failing had me feeling embarrassed and ashamed. I ended up getting in a fight that got me expelled from that school. At the next school, I became an honor roll student. Seeing my father feeling proud of me was a good feeling and I wanted to always make him feel good about being my dad. Proverbs 23 verse 24, "he that begetteth a wise child shall have joy of him." Proverbs chapter 17 verse 21, "A father of a fool has no joy."

As parents, the best thing we can do is train up our children in the way they should go. Proverbs chapter 22 verse 6. That's all we can do. Teach the bible, teach them good character, and teach them to be leaders is about all. We can keep them covered in prayer and pray they make good decisions. Sometimes our children may not mirror what we taught them. We as parents must not do anything that would cause our children to do wrong. I admit, there are those of us who didn't know how to be a parent, and made a lot of corrections along the way. As long as you did the best you could, don't be so hard on yourself. Ephesians chapter 6 verse 4, "And, ye fathers, provoke not your children to wrath: but bring them up in the nurture and admonition of the Lord." Even when we are upset or disappointed in our children, we must find a way to encourage them. We do not want to make the situation worse. If you brought them up in the nurture and admonition of the Lord, you did your job. If your children are giving you a hard time, you must cast these cares unto the Lord. I said this to my own son, "If you decide to become a criminal and go to prison, as much as that is going to hurt me, I'm going to cast my hurt to the Lord and live my life." The look on his face said it all. I know I did the best I could and that's all I can do as a parent. I can be at peace knowing I did my best.

If you didn't do the best you could, or if you had a child that you didn't want, repent, ask God to forgive you, and forgive yourself. Your child/children still have a will of their own. There are children who had terrible parents who made great decisions and I know of children who had great parents who made terrible choices. Once again, cast these cares on the Lord and allow the Lord to heal you. Let go of the guilt. Pray for your children and ask God to help them cast their cares on Him. Pray for them to receive the Lord or rededicate their lives to Him. We can all start over in the Lord and God can wipe the slate clean for us all. It's easy to have joy when our children are righteous and doing what we believe is right, but can we have joy even when are children decide to do wrong? Remember, joy is a fruit of the Holy Ghost within you. The hurt is real, but God can heal you and make you whole. Your children can have a new life in Christ after bad decisions and choices. Those weights, burdens, and sadness can all be replaced with healing, wholeness, and joy.

Prayer: (If you did your best.)

I thank you Lord for being a parent. I thank you that I did my best. I ask you to bless my child/children and lead them in the path that they should go. Let your holy angels protect them and help them make good choices. Lead them into prayer and let them seek your face for direction in their lives. Let us all be filled with your joy as we commune with you. Thank you Lord for all you've done for us all. I bless you. In Jesus name I pray. Amen.

Prayer: (If you didn't do your best or you didn't want your child/children.)

Father, I repent that I wasn't the best parent that I could be. I'm sorry that I wasn't there for my child/children, and I ask you to forgive me. From this day forward, I desire to be the best parent I can be and I ask you to show me how to be a parent to my children. Give me the

The Joy *of the* Lord

information and tools I need to parent my child/children. I ask you to heal my child/children over everything I failed to do, and I ask you Lord to help my child/children to forgive me. Help us all cast our cares on you and heal us as a family. Make us whole and order our steps together from this day forward. I thank you for our new start and we ask that your sweet comforting presence will manifest in all of our lives to bring unity between us. I give you glory and praise Lord. In Jesus name I pray. Amen.

Page | 107

-Day 16-

Joy In Judgment

I was very surprised to understand this verse in the bible once I became a more mature Christian. Proverbs is the one book I've read more than others. I used to read a chapter of Proverbs every day before I studied other books in the bible. "It is joy to the just to do judgment:" Proverbs chapter 21 verse 15. For many years I didn't understand this verse, but now I do. It makes sense that joy will be to those who judge people righteously. Why? Because God doesn't have respect of persons in His judgement of us. (Acts chapter 10 verse 34 & Romans chapter 2 verse 11) If you're wrong in the eyes of God, you're wrong. Your title of Apostle, Pastor, Evangelist, Prophet, Bishop, Deacon, or head of whatever, doesn't carry any weight with the Lord. You do not get a free pass to sin or to treat God's people (your members or followers) like they are beneath you, less than you, or nothing at all. Your obedience is necessary. Moses didn't make it into the promise land because of his disobedience. King David had to fight wars and deal with other things because of his sins. When we judge each other without respect of persons, God is pleased. Whether you believe it or not, people with titles are not sin free. We are all guilty of something, but there are times when people with titles do things and judge others with respect of persons. I've experienced this many times and seen it done to others plenty of times. Why is it that Christians don't want to believe their pastor is incapable of doing anything wrong? Your pastor is fallible and can make a choice to do something against the word of God. The one thing I've learned is most church leadership is guilty of respect of persons in judgement.

I thought of writing a book entitled, "Fickle Christians." In this book I would detail all of the respect of persons I've experienced in multiple churches through the years. There are church folks who believe everything people in church leadership say, namely their pastor and whoever their pastor endorses. Whatever they say it must be true because they are anointed. There are Christians that have good names, but they are guilty of respect of persons. There are pastors and prophets who are guilty. Bishops, deacons, ushers, church mothers, choir directors, praise and worship leaders, and respected members of churches; especially those who sit on the front row. I've sat on front rows, I've sat in pulpits, I've been an armorbearer, I've been an adjutant, I've been the head of the men's ministry, and I've been a praise and worship leader. I was the person appointed to pick up important people from the airport. I've been in multiple inner circles. As I write this book, this is year 30 in my Christian walk. When I say I've witnessed and experienced respect of persons, I truly mean it.

Cliques are within churches. There are pastors who refuse to allow certain members of their church to go forth in ministry. This is respect of persons. You're having secret meetings because you do not desire to invite certain people. This is respect of persons. You're purposely leaving out certain people from being knowledgeable of important information. This is respect of persons. Here is why people are leaving your church. God is sending them away because you wouldn't allow them to go forth in ministry. You wouldn't allow them to answer the call in your church. Now you're angry that God sent them away. What I just shared is respect of persons, but let's now dig into "respect of persons in judgement."

John chapter 7 verse 24, "Judge not according to the appearance, but judge righteous judgment." Jesus said these words. When it comes to issues in our churches, we are to judge righteous judgement. Be open to hearing both sides no matter who the two, or more, individuals are. If one of them is someone you look up and the other is someone you don't care for, can you judge righteously? I can. Can you? If the person you look up to is wrong, judge them as wrong. It doesn't matter how God uses them or what their position is. This is righteous judgement. Sin is sin, wrong is wrong, and right is right, no matter who is involved. A person's title should not influence how you're going to judge a situation. Remember, you are going to reap what you sow; even in judgment. I really hated being lied on publicly. I was wondering who was going to step up and do what the bible says concerning judging my situation. It happened publicly so I expected to see this judged publicly, but I never did. I had to let it go, and let God deal with the situation. God will remove all false reproaches and lies on our names in His timing. God reveals truth and He's doing it for me, and He will do it for you. I received several prophetic words concerning the public lies and they came on live social media from respected prophetic voices. It was so refreshing and comforting to know that the people of God heard from God in truth concerning my situation. In a nutshell, I was told God is going to reveal the truth. Amen.

Receiving bad judgments is painful, but it's important that we judge righteous judgement. God loves it. When we judge righteous judgment, God is pleased and blesses us with joy. You're going to feel great giving righteous judgment. It's all about the truth. It's not about the person you like better. Just because someone has a powerful anointing doesn't mean judge in their favor. Anointed people can sin, operate in respect of persons, and handle a situation wrong like anyone else. Please judge righteous judgement. Do not side with someone who is wrong. Tell them they are wrong in love and joy will be to you.

Prayer:

Lord, I ask you to purify my heart so I will judge righteous judgement. Please forgive me for operating in respect of persons (if necessary). I ask you to give me a strong spirit of discernment so I can judge ever matter righteously in truth. Let me judge all matters in your love and grace. Let the Holy Spirit within me lead me and guide me in all truth concerning judging any matter. Let my ear to hear truth be sharp and let me give your word in all judgments. I give you praise and glory. In Jesus name. Amen

-Day 17-

Reaping In Joy

I know if I sow joy, I will reap joy. I tell you, there have been times when I was dealing with something that had me severely heavy, and here comes a stranger releasing joy in my life. Sometimes it was a phone call from a joyful friend or associate. It's amazing when I received these phone calls, I really didn't want to answer. I'm so glad I did because their joy stirred up my joy. Joy can be very contagious if your heart is open to receiving laughter, jokes, and encouragement. You can definitely reject it. You can reject help, assistance, charity, love, family, friendship, and you can reject God. I've tried to encourage people who refused everything I was telling them. Depression, heaviness, and discouragement can have you rejecting those who desire to help you or minister to you. If you are in this place, you are bound and in need of deliverance. I've been in this place before and I refused phone calls from those who really cared about me. I didn't answer the door when they came knocking to check on me. I stayed off social media during this season and didn't respond to direct messages. I pushed people away and so grateful they were still there when I was finally delivered. Whenever you are isolated from those who care about you, you are in a dangerous place; especially if you stop going to church and ministry gatherings. Fortunately, while in this place, God is yet with you; even if you rejected Him, in rebellion, or angry at Him. Everyone in this place is there for different reasons. Life and situations affect us all differently. Nonetheless, God is faithful to us regardless. He will never leave us nor forsake us. Glory to God.

Maybe you're someone who hasn't sown joy to reap joy. Maybe you're that person who's life has been mostly negative and filled with bad experiences or traumas. As a member of the body of Christ, you have so many benefits that you must tap into. Study the gospels and learn about Jesus. Study verses on deliverance such as 2nd Corinthians verses 3 – 5. Your thought life must be transformed. Study Philippians chapter 4 verse 8. Even though you're hurting, start thinking on good things. Get back in the church. Call your friends and family. Get back in the game. Your time out is over.

Above all, remember this, "They that sow in tears shall reap in joy." Psalm 126 verse 5. During this season of your life, sow good things in your tears. Do what's right through your pain. Psalm 126 has an author who is talking about the captivity they experienced and how God turned it around for them. Verse 4 has the author asking God to turn their captivity again. Something happened and this person has found themselves bound again. They are asking God to set them free a second time. No one enjoys bondage. They are encouraged because the Lord delivered them before and they have faith God will do it again. In addition, this author says something very encouraging in verse 6. I love the fact that the author speaks to those who are weeping who are "bearing precious seed." Now the writer was talking about natural seed. If the weepers do not sow their precious seed, they will not reap a harvest. We as the children of the living God have plenty of things that we can sow. We are bearing lots of precious seed. God says whatever we sow we will reap. We can sow love although we are not loved. We can sow acceptance although we are rejected. We can sow compassion although we may not have anyone naturally who cares about us. Even though you may be going through a hard season in your life, you can sow good things in tears. You can do unto others as you desire them to do unto you in tears, and reap in joy. Now if there are people weeping who are bearing precious seed, we can also say there are people weeping who have no precious seed. What do I mean? These people are so focused on their situation that they do not care about anyone else. They only care about themselves. They have an inability to function without their life being a certain way. Their condition has them paralyzed. These are the people who will not say anything to encourage someone other than themselves. If they are in church leadership, they will not release the word of the Lord to you because of the condition of their life. God will give them a dream about someone and they will not share it. If you're this type of person, please come out of it. Please sow good seed in your tearful season. You will eventually reap a harvest of joy. "Sow to yourselves in righteousness, reap in mercy; break up your fallow ground; for it is time to seek the Lord, till he come and rain righteousness upon you."

Hosea chapter 10 verse 12

"but to him that soweth righteousness shall be a sure reward."

Proverbs chapter 11 verse 18.

Please sow your precious seed in your tearful seasons. You will reap in joy. The Lord promises you this. Your tearful season isn't forever. "For all the promises of God in him are yea, and in him Amen, unto the glory of God by us." 2nd Corinthians chapter 1 verse 20

There is a reward for you from God if you sow your precious seed. God values us doing what He loves and desires from us. It's time to seek the Lord. For those of you who have been paralyzed in your situation. Call your family and friends. Go back to church. Make yourself go somewhere you love. Speak life to yourself and to others. Encourage yourself and others. It's going to be ok. I've been there and done this myself. You got this. You'll reap joy. Joy is your portion. Joy is your reward. Hallelujah.

Prayer:

Lord, I thank you for your promises over my life. I ask you to heal my heart over the painful experiences of my life. I ask for your strength to sow precious seed so I can reap your joy. I ask you to help me seek your face, and focus my thoughts on things that are pure, righteous, holy, joyful, and funny. Help me to press my way through this season until I am reaping your joy. I praise you for my harvest of joy. In Jesus name I pray. Amen.

Hallelujah, bless the Lord!

About The Author

Marcus L. Boston is the owner of Unfazed Publishing LLC. He's been a published author since 2007 and shares his entire life in transparency to minister to others. He is a Christian of thirty years and has written many books to aid Christians in their walks with Christ. His first book, "A Pastor's Mistake. What To Do When You Know Your Pastor Is Wrong," sparked a lot of controversy and criticism. Marcus was attacked by various Christians thinking he was using real names and exposing people with personal attacks. After these Christians discovered that all names were changed and that the book was written respectfully, he began to get some better reviews.

His trademark in writing is being very transparent. He shares his life in truth in an effort to show non-Christians the grace that

God has for himself, is the same grace God has for them. He shares his failures in an effort to help others avoid the same pitfalls he experienced; especially those who didn't grow up in the church. His personal theme is "Making The Church A Better Place"

Contact Me

Would you like to book me for an appearance or speaking engagement? Would you like autographed books? Would you like to become an author with me? Please contact me.

info@unfazedpublishing.com

www.UnfazedPublishing.com

www.MarcusLBoston.world

224.762.2242

www.ingramcontent.com/pod-product-compliance
Lightning Source LLC
Chambersburg PA
CBHW060811050426
42449CB00008B/1627